JORDAN ELIAS

# Ethiopian Bible in English: The Complete 88-Book Collection

*The Ancient Scriptures of the Ethiopian Orthodox Church*

*This book is dedicated to all those who seek to understand the rich, sacred heritage of the Ethiopian Orthodox Church. May these ancient scriptures bring wisdom, peace, and a deeper connection to the divine. To the generations past who preserved these texts and to those who continue to share them with the world this work is for you.*

# Preface

The Ethiopian Bible, a treasure trove of spiritual wisdom and historical significance, holds a unique place in the Christian tradition. With its 88 sacred books, it presents a fuller picture of God's word as understood by the Ethiopian Orthodox Church. This collection not only includes familiar texts but also encompasses those ancient writings that have long been considered hidden or apocryphal by other branches of Christianity. The inclusion of books like The Book of Enoch and Jubilees gives this Bible a profound depth that enriches our understanding of the Christian faith.

In this book, I have made an effort to present the Ethiopian Bible in a way that is accessible to a wider audience, while still respecting its traditional roots. The text is translated with care to preserve the meanings and nuances embedded in the original scriptures. With each page, you are invited to discover more than just a collection of ancient writings; you are invited to explore a living faith that has sustained the Ethiopian people for centuries.

Whether you are new to the Ethiopian Bible or have studied it for years, I hope this book offers you fresh insights and a renewed sense of connection to the spiritual and historical richness of these sacred texts. May this journey through the pages of the Ethiopian Bible deepen your understanding, broaden your spiritual horizon, and inspire you to embrace the teachings of these ancient scriptures in your daily life.

# Acknowledgments

I would like to extend my heartfelt gratitude to all those who have supported me throughout the creation of this book. First and foremost, I thank the Ethiopian Orthodox Church for preserving and sharing the profound spiritual wisdom embedded within these sacred texts. Their unwavering dedication to the Ethiopian Bible has made it possible for us to experience and study this rich heritage.

To my family and friends, your encouragement and belief in this project have been invaluable. Your support, both emotional and practical, allowed me to stay focused on bringing this book to life.

I would also like to thank the scholars, translators, and historians whose work has made the translation of these ancient scriptures into English possible. Your expertise and commitment to accuracy ensured that the true meaning and depth of these texts are preserved for future generations.

To my readers whether you are new to the Ethiopian Bible or have long been a part of its tradition I am deeply grateful for your interest in this work. It is my hope that this book inspires a deeper understanding of the Ethiopian Bible's teachings and brings you closer to the divine wisdom that has shaped the lives of millions.

Lastly, I want to express my deepest gratitude to the community of Ethiopian Christians who have embraced this sacred collection for centuries. This book is a humble tribute to your faith, resilience, and unwavering commitment to preserving this treasure for the world.

# Introduction

## Understanding the Ethiopian Bible

### *The Significance of the Ethiopian Bible*

The Ethiopian Bible stands as a profound testament to the deep spiritual and cultural legacy of the Ethiopian Orthodox Church. It is not merely a collection of sacred texts, but a living embodiment of a faith tradition that has endured for over 1,500 years. Its place in Christian history is unique, as it preserves a version of the Christian scriptures that includes writings not found in most other Christian Bibles. This distinctiveness not only sets the Ethiopian Bible apart but also highlights the Church's commitment to preserving the full depth of Christian thought and practice through the centuries.

The Ethiopian Orthodox Church, one of the oldest Christian communities in the world, has maintained a remarkable devotion to these ancient texts. As one of the first regions in the world to officially adopt Christianity, Ethiopia became a crucial center of early Christian thought, and its scriptures reflect that rich heritage. Christianity was brought to Ethiopia in the 4th century by St. Frumentius, a Christian missionary who played a pivotal role in spreading the faith. Since then, the Ethiopian Church has carried a unique version of the Christian Bible, one that is marked by a wider range of sacred writings than that of the Western or Eastern Christian traditions.

This Bible, in its full 88-book canon, offers a broader, deeper understanding of the Christian faith. In a world where many Christian communities base their teachings on a standardized set of 66 books, the Ethiopian Bible's inclusion of additional texts highlights the diversity of early Christian thought and scripture. The Ethiopian Bible is a window into the past a reflection of an ancient faith that was preserved not only through centuries of theological development but also through political and cultural struggles. Through wars, invasions, and shifts in religious power, the Ethiopian Orthodox Church has kept its scriptures intact, never wavering from its commitment to the texts that have shaped the spiritual lives of its people.

The Ethiopian Bible is, therefore, a sacred gift—not only to Ethiopia but to the entire Christian world. It stands as a spiritual and cultural bridge between ancient Christianity and the modern world. For those who seek a deeper connection to the roots of Christian faith, the Ethiopian Bible offers a path of discovery and enlightenment. It is more than a book; it is a journey into the heart of one of the world's most ancient and enduring Christian traditions.

## The 88 Books

What truly sets the Ethiopian Bible apart from other Christian Bibles is its expansive collection of 88 books, a canon that is notably larger than those found in both Protestant and Catholic traditions. While most Christian Bibles contain 66 books 39 in the Old Testament and 27 in the New Testament the Ethiopian Bible includes several additional books, many of which have long been regarded as apocryphal or non-canonical by other Christian denominations. This unique arrangement of books not only defines the Ethiopian Bible but also offers a richer, more complete picture of the early Christian Church.

Among the books that distinguish the Ethiopian Bible are *The Book of Enoch*, *The Book of Jubilees*, *The Ascension of Isaiah*, *The Epistle of Barnabas*, *The Shepherd of Hermas*, and many others. These texts have provided early Christian communities with insights into prophecy, morality, the nature of the divine, and the life and teachings of Jesus Christ. They delve into subjects ranging from the nature of creation to the ultimate purpose of humanity and the universe. They offer detailed accounts of the lives of biblical figures, visions of the future, and interpretations of God's covenant with His people. For instance, *The Book of Enoch* is rich with angelology and cosmology, providing vivid descriptions of heavenly realms and the roles of angels in God's creation, which are themes that remain absent in most canonical scriptures.

Furthermore, *The Book of Jubilees* is often referred to as the "Little Genesis" because of its retelling of the events found in the Book of Genesis, but with additional layers of detail. It offers an expanded account of the patriarchs and the history of Israel, illuminating the early stories of the Bible with a fresh perspective. These writings provide a deeper, more complex view of God's dealings with His people, making the Ethiopian Bible an invaluable resource for understanding the foundations of Christian theology.

In addition to these extraordinary books, the Ethiopian Bible's Old Testament includes books like *1 Esdras*, *Tobit*, and *Judith*, which were once part of the Septuagint and are still considered canonical in the Ethiopian Orthodox tradition. These texts offer valuable insights into the Jewish traditions that were shared by early Christians, contributing to a richer understanding of the biblical narrative and its context.

This expanded canon provides readers with a more comprehensive understanding of biblical history and theology, offering both familiar and unfamiliar perspectives on the sacred scriptures. The Ethiopian Bible is a treasure trove of ancient knowledge, preserving texts that were integral to early Christian thought but were later excluded from many other Christian canons. For those who are seeking to understand the roots of Christian belief, the Ethiopian Bible serves as an indispensable resource that illuminates the theological and historical foundations of the faith.

## A Sacred Legacy

The preservation of the Ethiopian Bible is not just a matter of religious devotion, but an act of cultural and spiritual significance. The Ethiopian Orthodox Church has maintained these texts through centuries of turmoil, from the rise and fall of empires to the incursions of foreign powers. Despite challenges, the Church has always regarded the preservation of its sacred scriptures as essential to its identity and mission. The fact that these texts are still preserved and read in Ethiopia today is a testament to the Church's dedication to its spiritual and cultural heritage.

The importance of translating and sharing these ancient texts with the world cannot be overstated. By making the Ethiopian Bible available to a wider audience, we not only enrich the global understanding of Christianity, but also ensure that the wisdom and spiritual insights contained within these texts are passed on to future generations. The act of translating the Ethiopian Bible into English and other languages is a crucial step in making this sacred legacy accessible to people across the globe.

Moreover, as the world becomes more interconnected, there is a growing need to understand the diversity of Christian traditions. The Ethiopian Bible offers a window into a distinct Christian tradition that has much to contribute to the broader Christian community. Its teachings, history, and theology provide valuable insights that can enrich and deepen our understanding of God's word.

Preserving the Ethiopian Bible and making it accessible is an act of faith and scholarship. By translating these texts and sharing them with others, we are not only preserving the sacred heritage of the Ethiopian Orthodox Church but also offering the world a deeper connection to the history and teachings of the early Christian Church. As the Ethiopian Bible continues to be shared and explored, its legacy grows stronger, ensuring that this sacred collection of texts will continue to inspire and guide generations to come.

## *The Role of the Ethiopian Orthodox Church*

The Ethiopian Orthodox Church has played a central role in shaping not only Ethiopia's religious life but also its political, cultural, and social structures. From the moment that Christianity took root in Ethiopia, the Church became the cornerstone of Ethiopian civilization. It influenced the structure of the monarchy, the arts, the education system, and even daily life. The Church's authority was not limited to the religious realm but extended into governance, law, and ethics, with the clergy often involved in political matters and the king serving as the protector of the Church.

The Ethiopian Orthodox Church developed distinct practices early on, influenced by both local customs and the broader Christian traditions of the time, particularly those of the Egyptian and Eastern Orthodox Churches. One of the most significant early contributions of the Ethiopian Orthodox Church was its preservation of ancient Christian texts, many of which have been lost to other Christian traditions. The Church's focus on maintaining its sacred scriptures meant that Ethiopia became a repository for many early Christian writings that were either excluded from the canonical Bible or considered apocryphal in other parts of the Christian world.

The Ethiopian Orthodox Church also played a major role in the preservation of the Ge'ez language, an ancient language of Ethiopia that is still used in the liturgy of the Church today. Ge'ez is considered one of the oldest and most significant liturgical languages in Christianity, and it has been the vehicle through which Ethiopian Christian writings were preserved, including the Bible, hymns, prayers, and theological texts.

Beyond its liturgical language, the Ethiopian Orthodox Church fostered a rich artistic tradition that remains closely tied to Christian practice. Ethiopian religious art, particularly iconography, became renowned for its unique and deeply spiritual style, which emphasized vivid depictions of biblical scenes, saints, and angels. These works of art were not merely decorative but were seen as windows into the divine realm, helping believers connect with God in their worship. Ethiopian churches, built in both rural and urban areas, often feature striking religious art that is both visually and spiritually significant, with each painting or carving telling a biblical story or expressing an aspect of Ethiopian Christianity.

The Church also took on a central role in Ethiopian education and scholarship. Monasteries and churches became centers of learning, preserving not only Christian religious texts but also classical knowledge. Ethiopian scholars translated ancient works into Ge'ez, studied classical Greek and Latin texts, and preserved writings that would otherwise have been lost to history. The monastic tradition of the Ethiopian Orthodox Church produced many of the early manuscripts of the Bible, including some of the oldest surviving copies, which remain invaluable for scholars studying the history of the Christian faith and its development in Africa.

## The Development of the Ethiopian Canon

The development of the Ethiopian Bible's canon was a complex and gradual process that took place over several centuries. Unlike other Christian traditions, which typically accepted a fixed number of books as part of their official scripture, the Ethiopian Orthodox Church embraced a broader collection of texts that were seen as sacred. The recognition of these texts as canonical was influenced by theological debates, regional practices, and the Church's desire to preserve a more complete account of early Christian thought and history.

The Ethiopian canon consists of 88 books, including both well-known texts like the books of Genesis, Psalms, and the Gospels, as well as additional writings that were excluded from other Christian traditions. Among these additional books are *The Book of Enoch*, *The Book of Jubilees*, *The Shepherd of Hermas*, *The Ascension of Isaiah*, and *The Apocalypse of Peter*, which offer unique insights into early Christian theology and practice.

Many of these texts were considered apocryphal or non-canonical by other Christian denominations, particularly after the Council of Carthage in 397 CE, which solidified the canon of the Western Church. However, in Ethiopia, these books continued to be regarded as holy scripture, preserved by the Ethiopian Orthodox Church despite external pressures. *The Book of Enoch*, in particular, became one of the most significant of these additional texts. Its apocalyptic themes, visions of heaven and hell, and stories about fallen angels have captured the imagination of both religious and academic scholars. It offers an expanded narrative of biblical stories, including those of Noah and the fallen angels, and provides a unique perspective on God's plan for the world.

*The Book of Jubilees*, often referred to as the "Little Genesis," recounts the stories of the patriarchs with additional details not found in the traditional Genesis account. This text provides a unique interpretation of the creation story, offering fresh perspectives on early humanity's relationship with God and the role of divine law. The Ethiopian Church regarded *The Book of Jubilees* as a vital part of its theological heritage, and it remains central to the Church's understanding of the Hebrew Scriptures.

The finalization of the 88-book canon of the Ethiopian Bible occurred between the 5th and 6th centuries, though debates about which texts should be included continued into later centuries. The Ethiopian Church, while influenced by the broader Christian world, was deeply committed to preserving its unique traditions and the sacred texts that had been passed down for generations. This dedication ensured that the Ethiopian Bible would remain distinct, offering a fuller, richer account of the Christian faith than that found in most other traditions.

# Chapter 2

## The Unique Books of the Ethiopian Bible

### *The Old Testament*

T he Ethiopian Bible contains a vast and rich array of books, including a more expansive Old Testament than what is found in most other Christian traditions. It is a collection that spans across Jewish, Christian, and apocryphal traditions, offering a comprehensive and diverse perspective on the history of God's people. The Old Testament in the Ethiopian Bible includes not only the well-known books found in the Hebrew Bible but also additional writings that reflect the unique theological and historical heritage of Ethiopia.

The traditional books in the Ethiopian Old Testament largely align with the Septuagint (LXX), the Greek translation of the Hebrew Scriptures, which was used by early Christians in the eastern Mediterranean. The Septuagint was pivotal in the spread of Christianity in the early centuries and remains a foundational text for the Ethiopian Church. The Ethiopian Bible's Old Testament includes the standard books of the Hebrew Bible, such as Genesis, Exodus, Leviticus, Numbers, and Deuteronomy, as well as the Prophets (Isaiah, Jeremiah, Ezekiel, etc.), the Psalms, and historical books like Samuel, Kings, and Chronicles.

However, what sets the Ethiopian Bible apart is the inclusion of several other books not found in the Hebrew Bible or the Protestant Old Testament. For instance, books such as *1 Esdras*, *Tobit*, and *Judith* are integral parts of the Ethiopian canon. These books were part of the Septuagint tradition and were included in early Christian Bibles but were later excluded from the Protestant and Catholic canons.

*1 Esdras*, which retells the events of the rebuilding of the Temple in Jerusalem, is an important historical text that complements the Book of Ezra and provides additional insight into the post-exilic period. *Tobit* and *Judith*, both books of Jewish wisdom literature, offer moral teachings, piety, and faithfulness in the face of hardship, echoing themes found in the Psalms and Proverbs. These additional books present a more holistic view of the life of God's people during the times leading up to and following the Babylonian exile.

One of the most notable features of the Ethiopian Old Testament is the inclusion of *The Book of Enoch*, an ancient Jewish text that explores themes of angels, the cosmos, and the final judgment. The inclusion of this text in the Ethiopian Bible gives the Old Testament a richer, more expansive worldview, one that includes apocalyptic and eschatological visions not found in other Old Testament writings.

While many of these books were excluded from later versions of the Hebrew Bible, the Ethiopian Church has preserved them as part of the biblical canon. The Ethiopian Old Testament offers a more complete narrative of God's revelation to humanity, highlighting the diversity of sacred writings that were valued in the early Christian world.

## The Apocryphal Books

One of the most defining features of the Ethiopian Bible is the inclusion of several books considered apocryphal by most other Christian traditions. These texts, which were highly regarded by early Christians but eventually excluded from the Protestant and Catholic canons, hold special significance within Ethiopian Christianity. The Ethiopian Church continues to consider these apocryphal books as sacred and essential to understanding the full breadth of Christian revelation.

Among the most significant of these apocryphal books are *The Book of Enoch* and *The Book of Jubilees*, both of which have captured the imaginations of theologians, historians, and believers for centuries. These books offer a deeper understanding of the world of angels, demons, and heavenly realms, expanding on the brief references to these subjects found in the canonical texts.

*The Book of Enoch* is one of the most famous and influential apocryphal texts, providing a detailed narrative about the Watchers, angels who descend to Earth to teach humanity, only to fall from grace and corrupt mankind. The book explores the themes of divine judgment, the fate of sinners, and the eventual restoration of justice in the world. The apocalyptic visions contained in *The Book of Enoch* are echoed in the New Testament, particularly in the writings of the Apostle John in the Book of Revelation, as well as in other apocalyptic literature.

The Book of Enoch provides a unique vision of the end times, where divine judgment will come upon the earth, and those who have remained faithful to God will be rewarded. It gives additional context to the teachings of Christ, especially in regard to divine justice, the role of angels, and the fate of humanity.

*The Book of Jubilees* is another highly significant apocryphal text within the Ethiopian canon. Known as the "Little Genesis," it is an expanded retelling of the events described in the Book of Genesis, with a special emphasis on the role of the patriarchs. It includes additional details about Adam and Eve, Noah, Abraham, Isaac, and Jacob, offering a fresh perspective on the foundational figures of the Jewish and Christian faiths.

The *Book of Jubilees* presents a chronological framework of "jubilees" or periods of 49 years, and it traces the history of God's covenant with His people through these cycles. It provides insight into how the Hebrew calendar was understood by ancient Jews and how sacred history was organized in a cyclical pattern. This book is also significant in its focus on the importance of observing the law, particularly regarding festivals, sacrifices, and moral conduct.

These apocryphal books contribute a wealth of theological and historical information, shedding light on the early Christian worldview and the diverse ways in which Christians understood God's will. By including these books in the canon, the Ethiopian Church offers a more comprehensive narrative that ties together the Old Testament, the apocryphal literature, and the New Testament into one cohesive spiritual and historical tradition.

## The New Testament

The New Testament in the Ethiopian Bible follows the general structure of other Christian Bibles, but with some notable distinctions in terms of additional writings and the inclusion of other early Christian works. The Ethiopian New Testament includes the familiar Gospels of Matthew, Mark, Luke, and John, along with the Acts of the Apostles, the Pauline Epistles, and the

General Epistles.

The Gospels in the Ethiopian Bible hold particular significance because of their connection to the unique traditions of the Ethiopian Orthodox Church. These texts form the core of Christian teachings and provide an account of the life, death, and resurrection of Jesus Christ. The Gospels serve as the foundation for Christian worship, theology, and morality. However, while the four canonical Gospels remain central to Ethiopian Christianity, the Church also places great emphasis on the role of local traditions, liturgies, and hymns that have developed over the centuries.

The Pauline Epistles, including letters to the Corinthians, Romans, and Galatians, are also central to Ethiopian Christian thought. These letters offer important guidance on Christian living, salvation, and the role of the Church in society. The Ethiopian Church places significant weight on the theological concepts of grace, faith, and the power of Christ's resurrection, which are core themes in the Pauline writings.

However, one of the distinctive features of the Ethiopian New Testament is its inclusion of additional texts that are often omitted from other Christian canons. One such example is *The Shepherd of Hermas*, an early Christian text that provides moral and ethical guidance for believers. While *The Shepherd of Hermas* was considered canonical by some early Christian communities, it was later excluded from most Western canons. The Ethiopian Church, however, continues to hold it in high esteem.

Another unique feature of the Ethiopian New Testament is the inclusion of *The Epistle of Barnabas*, which offers a Christian interpretation of Jewish traditions and practices. The Epistle of Barnabas is a significant text for understanding how early Christians viewed the relationship between the Old and New

Testaments and how they navigated the complexities of their Jewish heritage.

The Ethiopian New Testament thus reflects the Church's commitment to preserving early Christian writings that shed light on the development of Christian theology and practice. By including these additional writings, the Ethiopian Bible presents a fuller picture of the early Church's beliefs, struggles, and triumphs.

# Chapter 3

## Key Themes and Messages in the Ethiopian Bible

T*heology and Spirituality: Understanding the Unique Theological Perspectives within the Ethiopian Canon*

The Ethiopian Bible presents a rich and distinctive theological framework that reflects both its ancient roots and its unique place within the broader Christian tradition. Unlike many other Christian Bibles, the Ethiopian canon includes not only the familiar texts of the Old and New Testaments but also a wealth of apocryphal and deuterocanonical books, each contributing to a broader and more intricate understanding of God's will, humanity's relationship with the divine, and the ultimate purpose of life.

One of the central theological perspectives in the Ethiopian Bible is the idea of divine transcendence the belief that God is wholly separate from the created world and yet intimately involved in it. The Ethiopian Church has long emphasized the mystery of God's being and the incomprehensibility of His nature, highlighting the tension between God's infinite holiness and His willingness to enter into the world through His Son, Jesus Christ. This divine paradox is often reflected in the worship practices of the Ethiopian Orthodox Church, where rich liturgies, hymns, and prayers highlight God's majestic holiness as well as His compassionate love for humanity.

Another key theological concept in the Ethiopian Bible is the divine-human relationship. This is most clearly articulated through the figure of Christ, who in Ethiopian thought is seen as both fully divine and fully human. His life, death, and resurrection are central to Ethiopian theology, with the Church placing a strong emphasis on His role as the Redeemer who came to bring salvation to all people, especially the poor, oppressed, and marginalized. Ethiopian Christians often view Christ not only as a divine figure of ultimate authority but as an intimate companion who walks alongside His followers, offering guidance and comfort.

The Ethiopian Church also places great importance on the intercession of the saints and the Virgin Mary. The idea of a heavenly community of saints, who are believed to pray on behalf of the living, is deeply ingrained in Ethiopian spirituality. Saints are often seen as spiritual guides and helpers, and their lives and works are celebrated through religious feasts, pilgrimages, and the veneration of relics. The Virgin Mary, often referred to as the Mother of Mercy, holds a particularly revered place in Ethiopian Christianity, with many theological works emphasizing her unique role in the salvation of humanity.

Moreover, the Holy Spirit is an essential part of the Ethiopian Church's theology. The Ethiopian Bible places particular emphasis on the work of the Holy Spirit in the life of the Church and the individual believer. The Spirit is seen as the agent of God's presence in the world, empowering believers to live

19

righteous lives, to heal the sick, and to continue the work of Christ. Ethiopian spirituality often expresses itself through a deep sense of reverence for the Holy Spirit, who is invoked during prayer and worship, believed to guide the faithful toward truth and salvation.

*Moral Lessons and Parables: Focusing on the Teachings of Christ and the Prophets*

The Ethiopian Bible, like other Christian scriptures, is filled with teachings, moral lessons, and parables that provide guidance for righteous living. However, the Ethiopian canon's richness lies not only in its theological insights but also in its practical guidance for daily life. These teachings, often found in the words of Christ and the writings of the prophets, emphasize the importance of love, humility, charity, and forgiveness virtues that lie at the heart of Ethiopian Christian ethics.

The parables of Jesus, found in the four Gospels, are central to the moral teachings of the Ethiopian Bible. These simple yet profound stories illustrate deep spiritual truths about God's kingdom, human nature, and the path to salvation. For example, the Parable of the Good Samaritan, which teaches the importance of loving one's neighbor, is not only a foundational ethical principle in Ethiopian Christianity but also a reflection of the Church's deep commitment to social justice and care for the poor and marginalized. This story, and others like it, highlight the importance of compassion, generosity, and the willingness to serve others, irrespective of social or cultural boundaries.

The Sermon on the Mount, in which Christ offers profound teachings on prayer, love, and forgiveness, is another key source of moral guidance in the Ethiopian Bible. Passages such as "Blessed are the poor in spirit" and "Blessed are the peacemakers" speak directly to the Ethiopian Christian ethos, which emphasizes humility, peace, and a deep reliance on God. These teachings are not just to be understood intellectually but are meant to shape the daily lives of believers, guiding them in how they treat others and live out their faith in the world.

In addition to the teachings of Christ, the prophets of the Old Testament also provide essential moral guidance. Prophets like Isaiah, Jeremiah, and Amos challenge the people of Israel and, by extension, the Ethiopian people to remain faithful to God's covenant and to live justly. These prophets condemn idolatry, social injustice, and the exploitation of the poor, while calling for repentance, humility, and a return to God. The Ethiopian Church has long held the prophetic books in high regard, and the lessons they impart about justice, righteousness, and fidelity to God continue to resonate in the Church today.

A unique feature of the Ethiopian Bible is its inclusion of books like The Book of Wisdom and The Shepherd of Hermas, which offer additional moral teachings and guidance. These texts present wisdom that encourages moral integrity, piety, and perseverance in the face of hardship. The Wisdom of Solomon, for example, speaks to the value of wisdom and understanding, and it underscores the importance of trusting in God's plan, even in the most difficult circumstances.

*Prophecies and Apocalyptic Visions: Insights from Books Like The Book of Enoch on the End Times and Divine Judgment*

One of the most striking features of the Ethiopian Bible is its rich apocalyptic and prophetic literature. These texts offer vivid descriptions of the end times, divine judgment, and the ultimate restoration of creation. The Ethiopian Bible's inclusion of apocryphal and deuterocanonical books like The Book of Enoch and The Apocalypse of Peter provides readers with a broader, more detailed understanding of biblical prophecy and eschatology.

The Book of Enoch, in particular, is one of the most important apocalyptic works in the Ethiopian canon. This text, which was considered sacred by early Christians but later excluded from most other Christian canons, presents a complex narrative of heavenly visions, divine judgment, and the fate of sinners. The book describes the fall of the angels, the rebellion of the Watchers (angels who descend to earth and corrupt humanity), and their subsequent punishment. The apocalyptic visions in Enoch depict a world on the brink of divine retribution, where the wicked will be judged and the righteous will be rewarded. These themes resonate deeply with the Ethiopian Christian understanding of justice, redemption, and the ultimate triumph of good over evil.

In The Book of Enoch, readers encounter a highly developed vision of the end times, where the Son of Man (a messianic figure) will return to judge the living and the dead. The book also introduces the concept of the final judgment, in which God will punish the wicked and reward the righteous. This concept of divine judgment and the ultimate triumph of God's kingdom is central to Ethiopian Christian eschatology. It offers hope to believers, assuring them that despite the suffering and injustice in the world, God's justice will prevail in the end.

Similarly, the Apocalypse of Peter presents a vision of the afterlife, showing the rewards for the righteous and the punishments for the wicked. This text, which was included in the Ethiopian Bible but excluded from most other canons, emphasizes the reality of divine judgment and the importance of living a righteous life in accordance with God's will. It offers vivid descriptions of heaven and hell, and it underscores the urgency of repentance and faith.

The apocalyptic writings in the Ethiopian Bible serve as both warnings and promises. They remind believers of the importance of living faithfully, trusting in God's justice, and awaiting the fulfillment of His promises. They also offer a vision of hope, where the faithful will be rewarded with eternal life, while the unjust will face the consequences of their actions.

# Chapter 4

The Language and Translation of the Ethiopian Bible

*The Ancient Languages: Amharic, Ge'ez, and the Significance of These Languages in the Preservation of the Bible*

The Ethiopian Bible is deeply intertwined with the ancient languages of Ethiopia, particularly **Ge'ez** and **Amharic**. These languages have played a crucial role in preserving the sacred texts and ensuring their continuity through the centuries. Understanding these languages is essential to understanding how the Ethiopian Bible has been passed down through generations and how its sacred teachings have been preserved and shared.

**Ge'ez**, an ancient South Semitic language, is the primary liturgical and classical language of the Ethiopian Orthodox Church. It is considered one of the oldest languages still in use today, with roots tracing back to the Kingdom of Aksum, where it served as both the language of administration and religion. Although Ge'ez is no longer a spoken language, it remains the language of worship, prayer, and theological discourse within the Ethiopian Church.

Ge'ez holds particular significance for the preservation of the Ethiopian Bible because it is the original language of many of the canonical and apocryphal books found in the Ethiopian canon. The **Old Testament**, **New Testament**, and several additional apocryphal texts were originally written in or translated into Ge'ez. These texts were passed down through oral and written traditions in the Ethiopian Orthodox Church, ensuring their integrity and continuity for centuries. Many early copies of the Ethiopian Bible were written in beautifully crafted manuscripts, often with elaborate illustrations and illuminations, which were preserved in monasteries and churches throughout Ethiopia.

While Ge'ez is no longer a spoken language, it remains central to the religious and cultural identity of Ethiopian Christians. The use of Ge'ez in the Ethiopian Church serves not only as a means of preserving ancient texts but also as a symbol of Ethiopia's deep spiritual connection to its Christian roots. The language's significance extends beyond its linguistic properties—it is a language of **divine revelation** and **sacred worship**, holding a unique place in the Ethiopian Christian experience.

**Amharic**, the official language of Ethiopia today, has played a significant role in the modern accessibility of the Ethiopian Bible. Amharic is a descendant of Ge'ez and serves as the primary language spoken by the majority of Ethiopians. In the 19th and 20th centuries, as Ethiopia began to modernize and expand its literacy efforts, the translation of religious texts, including the Bible, into Amharic became essential for the broader population. Amharic translations of the Ethiopian Bible made the sacred scriptures more accessible to people who spoke the language but were not familiar with Ge'ez.

The inclusion of Amharic as a language for Bible translation also helped to further integrate Christianity into the daily lives of Ethiopians. The language allowed people to engage more directly with the Bible and its teachings, thus fostering a deeper connection to the faith and enabling a greater understanding of God's word in their own cultural context. Today, the Ethiopian Bible is available in both Ge'ez and Amharic, providing Ethiopian Christians with the opportunity to study the Bible in both the original language of the Church and the modern language of their daily lives.

The transition from **Ge'ez** to **Amharic** and other languages like **English** reflects the Church's commitment to ensuring the Bible remains relevant and accessible to contemporary believers while also maintaining respect for the ancient traditions that have defined Ethiopian Christianity.

## *The Translation Process: How the Ethiopian Bible Was Translated into English and the Challenges Faced*

Translating the Ethiopian Bible into English has been a monumental task that has taken centuries to accomplish. The journey from the ancient Ge'ez texts to modern English has involved careful scholarship, a deep understanding of theology, and the need to balance accuracy with accessibility.

The first major translation of the Bible from **Ge'ez** into **European languages** occurred in the 17th century when Portuguese missionaries in Ethiopia began translating parts of the Bible into European languages. However, it was not until the 19th and 20th centuries that full translations into English became more widespread. The increasing interest in the Ethiopian Orthodox Church and its unique Christian heritage led scholars to focus on making the texts more accessible to a wider audience.

One of the most significant milestones in the translation

of the Ethiopian Bible into English was the work done by **Western scholars** in partnership with Ethiopian clergy and theologians. These collaborative efforts involved painstaking research to ensure that the original meanings of the texts were preserved, while also making them comprehensible to a non-Ge'ez-speaking audience.

The translation process faced several challenges. First, there was the issue of **language differences**. Ge'ez, while related to modern Ethiopian languages, is significantly different in structure, vocabulary, and grammar from both Amharic and English. Translating the rich theological concepts, metaphors, and cultural nuances of Ge'ez into English posed a substantial challenge. Many words and expressions in Ge'ez have no direct equivalents in English, making it necessary for translators to rely on context and theological understanding to accurately convey meaning.

Additionally, there were the challenges of **cultural translation**. The Ethiopian Bible is deeply tied to the culture, history, and traditions of Ethiopia. Some elements of the Ethiopian Christian worldview, such as the veneration of saints, the role of angels, and the unique theological interpretations of scripture, had to be explained in a way that would resonate with a broader Christian audience. Translating not only the language but also the cultural context of the Ethiopian Bible required careful attention to detail and a deep respect for the original texts.

Another challenge was the inclusion of the **apocryphal books** found in the Ethiopian Bible. Many of these texts, such as *The Book of Enoch* and *The Book of Jubilees*, are unknown to most Christian traditions outside of Ethiopia. Translating these books into English required an understanding of their theological importance and their connection to other biblical texts, as well as careful consideration of how to present them to readers unfamiliar with their content.

The efforts to make the Ethiopian Bible available in English have been ongoing, and while many parts of the Bible have been translated, the work continues. Modern translations aim to remain faithful to the original Ge'ez while also ensuring that the English version is accessible to contemporary readers. As new translations are completed and more scholarly work is done, the Ethiopian Bible will continue to evolve, ensuring that future generations of readers can engage with its teachings in their native languages.

## *Preserving Accuracy and Meaning: The Importance of Careful Translation to Preserve the Depth of the Text*

The translation of any sacred text is a delicate process, and translating the Ethiopian Bible into English is no exception. The importance of **preserving the accuracy and meaning** of the original texts cannot be overstated. The Ethiopian Bible contains profound theological concepts and historical narratives that have shaped the faith and spirituality of millions of believers. Therefore, ensuring that the translation maintains the depth and integrity of these texts is essential.

One of the central goals of translating the Ethiopian Bible is to **preserve the theological richness** found in the original Ge'ez texts. The Ethiopian Bible contains unique theological perspectives that are central to Ethiopian Christianity, such as the emphasis on the intercession of saints, the role of angels, and the apocalyptic visions found in texts like *The Book of Enoch*. It is important that these theological nuances are accurately translated into English, so that readers can fully appreciate the distinctiveness of Ethiopian Christian thought.

Equally important is the preservation of **cultural meaning**. The Ethiopian Bible is not simply a set of religious texts; it is a reflection of Ethiopian culture, history, and identity. As such, careful attention must be given to the cultural context of the scriptures. Translators must understand the cultural symbols, practices, and customs that are embedded within the text and make sure that these are conveyed clearly in English, without losing their significance.

At the same time, translations must ensure that the text remains **accessible and understandable** to readers who may not be familiar with the intricacies of Ethiopian theology or culture. This balance between **faithful translation** and **readability** is one of the primary challenges faced by translators. They must strike a careful balance, remaining true to the original while ensuring that the message of the text is communicated clearly and effectively to contemporary readers.

The **preservation of meaning** also extends to the apocryphal books, which are a crucial part of the Ethiopian Bible's distinctiveness. These books, while largely ignored or excluded in other Christian traditions, offer valuable insights into early Christian thought and spirituality. In the translation process, it is crucial that these texts are given the same level of attention and care as the more widely known books of the Bible. Translators must work to ensure that these texts are not simply seen as "extra" or "optional," but as integral parts of the biblical canon that offer a fuller and richer understanding of God's word.

Finally, the translation of the Ethiopian Bible is a work of **reverence**. Translators approach this task with great respect for the sacred nature of the text. The Ethiopian Bible is not just a historical document or a piece of literature; it is the very word of God, and the act of translation is an act of worship. As such, translators must approach their work with humility, seeking to preserve not only the accuracy of the text but also its divine inspiration.

# Chapter 5

## The Role of the Ethiopian Bible in Modern Faith

### *Impact on Ethiopian Orthodox Christianity*

T he Ethiopian Bible holds a central place in the lives of Ethiopian Orthodox Christians. It is not just a religious text; it is a living presence that shapes their daily lives, guides their worship, and influences their sense of community. The Bible is a key part of the spiritual foundation upon which Ethiopian society is built, and its role in everyday life cannot be overstated.

In the **daily life** of an Ethiopian Orthodox Christian, the Bible is a constant companion. From childhood, Ethiopians are taught to revere the Scriptures, and its verses are memorized and recited during prayer, rituals, and personal devotions. The Bible's influence extends into almost every aspect of life—from the way people greet each other with blessings, to how they approach work, family, and social responsibilities. For many Ethiopians, the teachings of the Bible are not abstract ideas, but practical guides for living out their faith in the world. They are reminded of the importance of humility, charity, and justice, and these principles are often put into practice through acts of kindness and care for others.

In **worship**, the Ethiopian Orthodox Church places great emphasis on the Bible as the foundation of Christian faith. Every service, whether it is a daily prayer or the grand celebrations of feasts and liturgical events, revolves around readings from the Bible. The liturgy of the Ethiopian Church is an elaborate, multi-sensory experience, and the Bible is at the heart of it. The scriptures are sung in Ge'ez, chanted by priests and deacons, and woven into the hymns and prayers that form the Church's daily rhythm. The act of hearing the Word of God read aloud in the Church is seen as a moment of direct communion with God, a means of receiving divine wisdom and guidance.

The Ethiopian Bible is also an essential part of the **sacraments** that are central to Ethiopian Orthodox Christianity. In particular, the Bible is crucial to the sacrament of **baptism**, **holy communion**, and **weddings**, where scripture readings provide the theological foundation for each sacred act. During baptisms, the names of saints, prophets, and biblical figures are invoked, and passages from the Bible are read to bless the child and initiate them into the Christian community. In the celebration of the **Eucharist** (holy communion), the Bible's teachings on the body and blood of Christ are honored, and the faithful participate in the mystery of the sacrament, grounded in the scriptural understanding of Christ's life and sacrifice.

The Bible's role in the **community** is just as significant. The Ethiopian Orthodox Church views itself not only as a place of individual spiritual growth but as a communal institution that unites believers in worship and fellowship. The shared experience of hearing scripture read aloud in the Church, participating in liturgical celebrations, and discussing the Bible in religious education classes helps strengthen the bonds of community. Whether in rural villages or urban centers, the Ethiopian Church serves as a source of moral guidance and spiritual unity, and the Bible is the touchstone of this shared faith.

In times of crisis or celebration, the Ethiopian Bible remains a source of comfort and strength for the community. Its verses provide solace during moments of grief, hope during hardship, and joy during festivals. The Ethiopian people, through the teachings of the Bible, are reminded of the transcendent love of God, which binds them together as a community and provides them with the strength to face the challenges of life.

## A Global Influence: How the Ethiopian Bible Is Respected and Revered by Non-Ethiopian Christians Worldwide

Though it has its origins in Ethiopia, the influence of the Ethiopian Bible has spread far beyond its borders, earning respect and reverence among non-Ethiopian Christians worldwide. Its inclusion of the 88 books, many of which are considered apocryphal or non-canonical by other Christian denominations, offers a broader and more inclusive view of Christian history and scripture. As a result, the Ethiopian Bible has become a **source of fascination** and **respect** for scholars, theologians, and religious communities around the globe.

One of the key aspects of the Ethiopian Bible that has drawn attention from global Christianity is the **Book of Enoch**. This apocalyptic text, with its vivid descriptions of angels, heavenly realms, and divine judgment, has captured the imagination of Christian scholars and mystics throughout history. It offers unique insights into the early Christian understanding of the nature of angels, demons, and the end times—topics that are briefly mentioned in other canonical texts but explored in much more detail in the Ethiopian Bible. For scholars of Christian history and theology, the Ethiopian Bible's inclusion of *The Book of Enoch* offers valuable insights into the diverse views of early Christian communities and their beliefs.

Beyond scholarly interest, the **Ethiopian Orthodox Church** itself has gained recognition and respect in the broader Christian world. Its ancient heritage, its commitment to preserving early Christian writings, and its deeply spiritual and vibrant liturgical practices have garnered admiration from many Christian denominations. **Ethiopian Christianity** has become a symbol of **faithful preservation**, standing as a bridge between early Christianity and modern Christian thought. Many non-Ethiopian Christians look to the Ethiopian Church as a model of **spiritual endurance**—a Church that has remained true to its ancient traditions while continuing to engage meaningfully with contemporary issues.

In recent years, there has been growing interest in the Ethiopian Bible among non-Ethiopian Christian communities, particularly those interested in exploring the **roots** of their faith. The 88-book canon, with its unique inclusion of apocryphal and deuterocanonical books, offers a fuller understanding of Christian history, theology, and eschatology. For many Christians outside Ethiopia, the Ethiopian Bible provides an opportunity to engage with early Christian writings that have been marginalized or overlooked by other Christian traditions.

*The Bible in the Modern Age: How Modern Technology Is*
*Helping Preserve and Share the Ethiopian Bible*

In the modern age, the role of technology has become increasingly important in the preservation and dissemination of
religious texts. The Ethiopian Bible, like many sacred scriptures,
has benefitted from advances in technology that allow it to be
shared and studied by a broader audience than ever before. From
digital archives to online translations, technology is playing a
vital role in ensuring that the Ethiopian Bible remains accessible
to believers around the world.

One of the most significant ways that technology is preserving the Ethiopian Bible is through the **digitization of ancient manuscripts**. The Ethiopian Orthodox Church has a
long tradition of preserving religious texts in the form of
handwritten manuscripts, many of which are ornately decorated
and contain ancient theological insights. With the advent of
digital archiving and scanning technology, these manuscripts
can now be preserved in a digital format, ensuring that they are
protected from the ravages of time, wear, and climate. Many
of these manuscripts, once stored in monasteries or private
collections, can now be accessed by scholars, theologians, and
the general public, making it easier to study and understand the
depths of the Ethiopian Bible's teachings.

Furthermore, **digital translations** of the Ethiopian Bible into
various languages have made it possible for people outside of
Ethiopia to access and study these sacred texts. The translation
of the Ethiopian Bible into languages like English, French, and
Arabic has allowed it to reach a global audience, enabling non-
Ethiopian Christians to engage with the richness of Ethiopian
Christianity. Online platforms and digital libraries now provide

access to the Ethiopian Bible and its many apocryphal books, making it easier for readers to explore the text from anywhere in the world.

The rise of **online education** has also made it possible for people to learn about the Ethiopian Bible in greater depth. Through online courses, virtual Bible studies, and digital lectures, individuals can now explore the theological, historical, and cultural significance of the Ethiopian Bible in a way that was once reserved for scholars or religious leaders. This democratization of knowledge has helped spread awareness of the Ethiopian Bible and its unique place within the global Christian community.

Additionally, **social media platforms** have played an essential role in raising awareness of the Ethiopian Bible, especially among younger generations. Social media has allowed Ethiopian Christians to share their faith, worship practices, and theological insights with a global audience, fostering a sense of community among believers from different cultures and traditions. Through platforms like Facebook, Instagram, and YouTube, Ethiopian Christians are able to engage with people from around the world, sharing their scriptures and teachings in ways that were not possible just a few decades ago.

The accessibility of the Ethiopian Bible in the modern age is not only a matter of preserving an ancient tradition but also an opportunity to connect with a new generation of believers who are eager to learn from the past while facing the challenges of the present. As modern technology continues to evolve, the Ethiopian Bible will likely remain at the forefront of efforts to preserve and share the timeless message of faith, hope, and salvation that it contains.

# Chapter 6

## The Beauty of Ethiopian Christian Art and Literature

*Iconography and Sacred Art: Exploring the Relationship Between Ethiopian Art and the Biblical Narrative*

Ethiopian Christian art is not just an aesthetic pursuit; it is a profound form of spiritual expression that reflects the essence of the Ethiopian Orthodox Church's theology, identity, and connection to the divine. From its earliest origins, Ethiopian Christianity has produced sacred art that is deeply rooted in biblical narratives, ancient traditions, and the teachings of the Church Fathers. The relationship between Ethiopian art and the Bible is unique—these artworks are not mere representations of biblical figures and stories but are viewed as **windows into the divine realm**, meant to foster a deeper spiritual connection with God and to invite believers to enter into the mysteries of the faith.

At the heart of Ethiopian Christian art is the **icon**. Ethiopian icons are visual expressions of the sacred, traditionally painted on wooden panels and created with an emphasis on **symbolism** and **spiritual depth**. The icons themselves are considered

**holy objects**, not merely artistic representations, and they are believed to contain the **presence of the saint or divine figure** they portray. Unlike Western Christian art, which often emphasizes realism and three-dimensionality, Ethiopian icons are characterized by their **flatness** and **vivid use of color**. Figures in Ethiopian icons are often depicted with exaggerated proportions, large almond-shaped eyes, and elongated bodies, reflecting the divine nature of the subjects and conveying the sense of eternal presence rather than temporal reality.

The faces in Ethiopian Christian art are often marked by **large, expressive eyes**, symbolizing spiritual vision and insight into the mysteries of the heavenly realm. These large eyes are not simply aesthetic choices; they are a reflection of the belief that the saints, angels, and biblical figures portrayed in the icons are **witnesses to the eternal truth** and have an intimate relationship with God. The **halo**, a common feature in Ethiopian icons, serves as a symbol of holiness and divine light, indicating that the depicted figure is filled with the grace and presence of God. These images create an atmosphere of reverence and prayer, inviting the viewer to look beyond the material world and into the divine mystery.

The **biblical narrative** is the primary source of inspiration for Ethiopian iconography. Icons often depict scenes from the **life of Christ**, such as the **Nativity**, the **Crucifixion**, and the **Resurrection**, as well as significant events from the **Old Testament**, like the **Creation**, the **Flood**, and the **Exodus**. These scenes are not merely illustrations of biblical stories but are meant to provide the faithful with an opportunity for spiritual reflection and meditation. For instance, the **Crucifixion** is often depicted in a way that highlights Christ's victory over death and the hope of resurrection, offering the believer not just a reminder of Christ's sacrifice but an invitation to experience the **redemptive power of the Cross**.

What makes Ethiopian Christian art unique is its focus on both **biblical figures** and **Ethiopian saints**, whose lives are intertwined with the divine narrative. Figures such as **St. Tekle Haymanot**, **St. Yared**, and **St. Abbo**—all of whom played pivotal roles in Ethiopian Christian history—are frequently depicted in Ethiopian icons. These saints, revered for their holiness and devotion, are shown as **mediators** between the human and divine, and their depictions in icons serve as models for the faithful to emulate. By including these local saints in the biblical narrative, Ethiopian Christian art emphasizes the continuity of the Church's divine mission and its grounding in **Ethiopian identity**.

In addition to icons, **Ethiopian mural art** plays an important role in the religious life of the Church. Painted murals often adorn the walls of **churches and monasteries**, depicting biblical stories, scenes from the lives of saints, and images of angels and Christ. These murals, like icons, are not only for aesthetic purposes but are meant to **transform the church space into a reflection of the divine**. The vibrant colors and intricate patterns of these murals engage the viewer's senses and encourage a sense of awe, while also providing a teaching tool to instruct the faithful in the doctrines of the faith. Ethiopian religious art is meant to be **immersive**, inviting the viewer to step into a world where the divine and the earthly intersect.

Ethiopian Christian art's deep connection to the **biblical narrative** elevates it beyond mere decoration—it becomes an integral part of the **worship experience**, helping the faithful to visualize and contemplate the stories that shape their spiritual lives. It serves not only as an educational tool but also as a

**spiritual guide** that invites all who view it to partake in the sacred mysteries and to draw closer to the divine.

*Literature Inspired by the Bible: A Look at Classic Ethiopian Religious Literature That Draws from the Bible*

Just as Ethiopian art is deeply connected to the Bible, so too is Ethiopian literature. The Ethiopian literary tradition has a rich and ancient history, with texts that draw directly from the Bible, as well as from other religious sources. Ethiopian literature serves as a vehicle for **spiritual reflection**, **theological exploration**, and the **preservation of biblical teachings** in a cultural context. From hymns and prayers to historical chronicles and theological treatises, Ethiopian literature has continually drawn from the Bible to shape the spiritual lives of the Ethiopian people.

One of the most significant forms of Ethiopian religious literature is **hymnography** the creation of sacred songs and hymns that are sung in praise of God and the saints. Many of these hymns are directly inspired by the Bible, reflecting on biblical themes such as God's majesty, the salvation brought by Christ, and the intercession of the Virgin Mary. **The Hymn of the Cherubim**, for example, is a famous Ethiopian liturgical hymn that expresses the eternal praise of God by the heavenly hosts, drawing from passages in the Old and New Testaments that describe the worship of God in heaven. Ethiopian hymns are often sung in **Ge'ez**, the ancient liturgical language of the Church, and their poetic language and melodic structure reflect the deep **reverence** and **devotion** with which Ethiopians approach the Scriptures.

In addition to hymns, **Ethiopian religious literature** also includes **theological works**, **sermons**, and **biblical commentaries** that draw from the Bible's teachings. **The Kebra Nagast** ("The Glory of the Kings") is one of Ethiopia's most famous and influential religious texts. While not part of the Bible, the Kebra Nagast recounts the legendary story of the Queen of Sheba's visit to King Solomon, the birth of their son Menelik I, and the establishment of the Solomonic dynasty in Ethiopia. The text connects Ethiopia's royal lineage to the biblical line of David, asserting the sacred nature of the Ethiopian monarchy and Ethiopia's unique status as the **New Jerusalem**. Though not included in the canon, the Kebra Nagast is an important text for understanding Ethiopia's Christian identity and its relationship to the biblical narrative.

Another essential text in Ethiopian Christian literature is **The Fetha Nagast** ("The Law of the Kings"), a comprehensive legal and moral code that was inspired by biblical teachings and established the relationship between the Church and the state. The Fetha Nagast draws extensively from biblical principles of justice, righteousness, and morality, offering guidance on issues such as governance, personal conduct, and social responsibility. It emphasizes the need for a righteous king who upholds God's laws and administers justice to the people, reinforcing the biblical idea that rulers are stewards of God's will on earth.

The **Book of the Covenant** and **the lives of saints** are also significant parts of Ethiopian religious literature. The lives of Ethiopian saints, often written in the form of hagiographies, recount the miraculous deeds, spiritual journeys, and moral lessons of saints who are revered within the Ethiopian Orthodox Church. These saints often draw inspiration from biblical figures and narratives, and their lives provide models of Christian virtue. Saint **Tekle Haymanot**, for instance, is revered for his unwavering faith and commitment to monastic life, and his hagiography tells of his miraculous healing powers and his efforts to spread Christianity in Ethiopia.

The writings of **Ethiopian theologians** and **church fathers**, such as **Abbo** and **St. Yared**, also draw from the Bible. St. Yared, in particular, is credited with creating the **Ethiopian Church's sacred music** and is often depicted in Ethiopian literature as a figure who brought the teachings of the Bible to life through music, inspiring Ethiopians to worship God through song and chant.

Ethiopian literature offers a **rich tapestry** of stories, prayers, hymns, and theological reflections that bring the Bible to life in the Ethiopian context. This literature serves as both a **spiritual guide** and a **cultural repository**, preserving the teachings of the Bible while also shaping Ethiopian identity and culture.

# Chapter 7

Comparing the Ethiopian Bible with Other Christian Bibles

*Canon Differences: A Comparative Analysis of the Ethiopian Bible and Other Christian Bibles, Focusing on Differences in the Old and New Testaments*

The Ethiopian Bible stands as one of the most distinctive Christian canons in the world, both in terms of its **size** and **content**. Unlike the Bible used by most Protestant, Catholic, and Eastern Orthodox Christian traditions, the Ethiopian Bible includes **88 books**, making it significantly larger. This expanded canon incorporates additional Old and New Testament books that are not found in the canonical collections of other Christian denominations. Understanding these differences is crucial to appreciating the unique place of the Ethiopian Bible within Christian history and theology.

**The Old Testament:**

The Ethiopian Old Testament includes all the books found in the **Hebrew Bible**, as well as additional books that are either apocryphal or deuterocanonical in other Christian traditions.

The standard **Protestant Old Testament** contains 39 books, while the **Catholic Old Testament** includes 46. The Ethiopian Old Testament, however, contains **more than 50 books**, with additional writings that have been preserved by the Ethiopian Orthodox Church since ancient times.

One of the most notable differences between the Ethiopian Old Testament and those of other Christian Bibles is the inclusion of books like **1 Esdras**, **Tobit**, **Judith**, and **The Wisdom of Sirach** (Ecclesiasticus), which are not found in the Protestant Bible but are included in the **Septuagint**, the Greek translation of the Hebrew Scriptures. The **Book of Enoch**, one of the most significant apocryphal works, is another key text in the Ethiopian Old Testament that is entirely absent from the Hebrew Bible, the Catholic Bible, and most Protestant Bibles. *The Book of Enoch* is an important source of apocalyptic imagery and is cited by early Christian writers, including **Jude** in the New Testament. Its vivid depictions of angels, the divine judgment, and the end of times have made it an influential text for Christian eschatology, especially in Ethiopian Christianity.

In addition to these texts, the **Ethiopian Bible** includes books like **Jubilees**, **The Book of the Covenant**, and **The Ascension of Isaiah**, which have had significant theological and historical importance in the Ethiopian Orthodox tradition. *The Book of Jubilees* is sometimes referred to as the "Little Genesis" because it retells the story of creation and the patriarchs with additional details and a focus on **divine law**. The Ethiopian inclusion of such writings offers a **broader and more diverse view** of Old Testament history and theology.

The **Protestant Bible** traditionally excludes these additional books, reflecting the Reformation-era move to standardize the Christian canon and reject writings that were not considered part of the Hebrew Scriptures. The **Catholic Bible**, while it includes some apocryphal books not found in Protestant Bibles, still does not embrace the full Ethiopian canon. This makes the Ethiopian Old Testament uniquely expansive, offering a more comprehensive and nuanced understanding of the Jewish and early Christian worlds.

**The New Testament:**

The Ethiopian New Testament, like other Christian canons, contains the four **canonical Gospels**—Matthew, Mark, Luke, and John—as well as the **Acts of the Apostles** and the **Pauline Epistles**. However, what sets the Ethiopian New Testament apart is the inclusion of additional writings that were widely read in the early Christian world but were later excluded from most Western canons.

One such text is the **Shepherd of Hermas**, an early Christian writing that deals with repentance, forgiveness, and the importance of living a righteous life. While it was highly regarded by early Christian communities and was included in some early Christian Bibles, it was later excluded from the Protestant and Catholic canons. Similarly, the **Epistle of Barnabas**, a letter that provides a Christian interpretation of Jewish customs and law, is found in the Ethiopian New Testament but is absent from most other canons.

Another key text in the Ethiopian New Testament is the **Book of the Covenant** (*Fetha Nagast*), which addresses the ethical and legal dimensions of Christian life. This book is not part of the New Testament in other Christian Bibles, but it holds a special place in Ethiopian Christianity, serving as a guide for Christian moral and ethical conduct.

The Ethiopian New Testament, like its Old Testament, preserves writings that reflect the early Church's diverse theological and spiritual currents. These writings help provide a more complete picture of early Christianity, offering insights into the development of Christian doctrine and practice in the centuries following Christ's resurrection.

*Spiritual Significance: How the Ethiopian Bible Offers a Unique View of Christianity and What It Contributes to Global Christian Thought*

The Ethiopian Bible offers a distinctive view of Christianity, one that integrates **rich theological insights**, **biblical traditions**, and **spiritual practices** unique to the Ethiopian Orthodox Church. It is a Bible that reflects the **church's deep commitment** to preserving ancient Christian teachings while also adapting to the cultural and historical realities of Ethiopia. This unique perspective offers valuable contributions to global Christian thought, especially in its approach to **scripture**, **tradition**, and **theological reflection**.

**Theological Diversity and Depth:** The Ethiopian Bible presents a **broader theological narrative** than many other Christian Bibles, incorporating not only the traditional biblical canon but also apocryphal texts that are deeply influential in Ethiopian Christianity. This **expansive canon** offers a **more inclusive understanding** of Christian faith, one that acknowledges the richness of early Christian writings that were once widely read and respected but later excluded from other Christian traditions. This diversity of texts offers a fuller understanding of Christian history, theology, and the evolution of early Christian beliefs.

For example, the **Book of Enoch**, which describes the fall of the angels and the coming judgment, adds an **apocalyptic**

**dimension** to the Ethiopian Bible that is not found in the traditional Protestant or Catholic Bibles. Its inclusion enriches the biblical understanding of **heavenly realms**, **divine judgment**, and the **cosmic battle** between good and evil. Similarly, the **Book of Jubilees** offers a more structured view of history, placing emphasis on **divine law** and the covenant between God and His people. These texts contribute to the broader **theological conversation** on the nature of God's relationship with humanity and the unfolding of salvation history.

**Ethiopian Christianity's Unique Spirituality:** One of the key contributions of the Ethiopian Bible to global Christianity is its emphasis on **mysticism** and **spiritual experience**. Ethiopian Christianity has long been characterized by a deep connection to the divine through the **liturgy**, **sacred art**, **fasting**, and **prayer**. The Ethiopian Bible's **focus on sacred rituals**, combined with its ancient canon, provides a **spiritual framework** that emphasizes **direct communion with God**, both in **individual devotion** and in **communal worship**.

The Ethiopian emphasis on the **intercession of saints** and the **veneration of Mary** highlights a unique aspect of Christian spirituality that complements the mainstream Christian focus on Christ. In the Ethiopian tradition, the **Virgin Mary** is seen not only as the mother of Jesus but as a **spiritual mother** to all believers, offering intercession and protection. This Marian devotion, along with the reverence for Ethiopian saints like **St. Tekle Haymanot** and **St. Yared**, shapes the unique spiritual landscape of Ethiopian Christianity and offers a deeper connection to the **heavenly realm**.

**Biblical Literalism vs. Symbolism:** Another important aspect of the Ethiopian Bible's spiritual significance is its approach to **biblical interpretation**. Unlike many other Christian traditions that emphasize a literal reading of the Bible, Ethiopian Christianity often leans toward **symbolic and allegorical** interpretations of scripture. This allows for a deeper spiritual understanding of biblical events and teachings, where the **spiritual truths** behind the texts are emphasized rather than a rigid, literal understanding of every word.

For example, the Ethiopian Orthodox Church places great significance on the **spiritual meaning** of Christ's **Passion**, seeing it as the key to unlocking the mysteries of salvation. This focus on **mystical interpretation** allows believers to engage with the Bible in a way that is **personally transformative**, inviting them to enter into the **mysteries of faith** and experience divine grace in everyday life.

**Global Contributions and Ecumenical Dialogue:** The Ethiopian Bible contributes significantly to **ecumenical dialogue** by offering a fuller understanding of Christian history and theology. Its diverse canon and its **spiritual richness** provide an important perspective on the early Christian tradition that is often missing from other biblical traditions. By sharing the Ethiopian Bible with the broader Christian world, the Ethiopian Orthodox Church invites other Christians to **reflect on their own understanding** of scripture and to engage with the **history of Christian thought** in a more inclusive and comprehensive way.

Ethiopia's long-standing role as a **preserver of ancient Christian texts** makes the Ethiopian Bible an important source for scholars and theologians worldwide. It offers valuable insights into the early Christian communities that existed before the split between Eastern and Western Christianity and offers a more **comprehensive narrative** of the Bible that spans across many different Christian traditions.

# Chapter 8

## Understanding the 88 Books: A Book-by-Book Breakdown

The Ethiopian Bible is unique not only because of its size but also because of the **richness and diversity** of the books it contains. With 88 books in total, the Ethiopian Bible offers a **comprehensive** and **detailed account** of Christian history, theology, and spirituality. These books include both well-known canonical books, as well as apocryphal and deuterocanonical texts that are preserved uniquely within the Ethiopian tradition. In this chapter, we will explore each of these books, summarizing their content, highlighting the key characters and stories, and discussing their theological significance.

*Book Summaries: A Concise Yet Insightful Summary of Each Book in the Ethiopian Bible*

## The Old Testament

- Genesis
- *Genesis* tells the story of creation, the fall of humanity, the flood, and the early history of Israel. It includes the accounts of Adam and Eve, Noah, Abraham, and Joseph. The foundational themes of God's creation of the world, humanity's fall into sin, and the promises made to the patriarchs are established here.
- Exodus
- *Exodus* focuses on the liberation of the Israelites from Egyptian slavery under the leadership of Moses. It includes the giving of the Ten Commandments, the establishment of the covenant, and the building of the Tabernacle. It's a key book for understanding God's deliverance and faithfulness to His people.
- Leviticus
- This book outlines the Levitical laws that govern Israel's worship and purity. It emphasizes holiness, sacrifices, and ritual laws. Aaron and the priesthood are central figures here, with a focus on how the people are to approach God in reverence.
- Numbers
- *Numbers* recounts the journey of the Israelites in the wilderness. It includes censuses, laws, and stories of rebellion and God's provision. The book highlights God's faithfulness despite Israel's struggles and disobedience.
- Deuteronomy

- A series of speeches by Moses before his death, *Deuteronomy* recaps Israel's history, laws, and covenant with God. It calls the people to faithfulness as they prepare to enter the Promised Land.
- Joshua
- *Joshua* narrates the conquest of the Promised Land under Joshua's leadership. The book emphasizes obedience to God's commands as the Israelites take possession of Canaan.
- Judges
- The book describes the period of the judges, when Israel was led by individuals like Deborah, Gideon, and Samson. This era is marked by cycles of sin, oppression, repentance, and deliverance.
- Ruth
- *Ruth* is the story of a Moabite woman who shows loyalty to her mother-in-law, Naomi, and later marries Boaz, a relative of Naomi's husband. The book showcases themes of faithfulness, redemption, and God's providence.
- 1 Samuel
- This book details the rise of Samuel, Israel's last judge, and the establishment of the monarchy with Saul as Israel's first king. It introduces David, who would become the second king, anointed by God.
- 2 Samuel
- *2 Samuel* chronicles the reign of David as king, his successes and failures, and the challenges of ruling Israel. It also details the Davidic Covenant, promising that David's descendants would rule forever.
- 1 Kings
- This book begins with the reign of Solomon and the con-

struction of the Temple in Jerusalem. It recounts the division of the kingdom after Solomon's death, leading to the split between the northern kingdom of Israel and the southern kingdom of Judah.

- 2 Kings
- 2 *Kings* continues the history of the divided kingdom, focusing on the reigns of various kings of Israel and Judah and the eventual fall of both kingdoms Israel to the Assyrians and Judah to the Babylonians.
- 1 Chronicles
- This book revisits the genealogies of Israel, focusing particularly on the reign of David and his preparations for the building of the Temple.
- 2 Chronicles
- 2 *Chronicles* continues the history of Judah, emphasizing the reigns of Solomon and the kings of Judah. It focuses on temple worship, the kingship, and the importance of fidelity to God.
- Ezra
- *Ezra* tells of the return of the exiled Israelites from Babylon and the rebuilding of the Temple in Jerusalem. Ezra leads the effort to restore religious practices and the observance of the law.
- Nehemiah
- *Nehemiah* focuses on the rebuilding of Jerusalem's walls and the restoration of Jewish identity in the post-exilic period, under Nehemiah's leadership.
- Esther
- The story of Esther, a Jewish queen in the Persian Empire, who saves her people from destruction through her courage and wisdom. Themes of divine providence and deliverance

are central to the book.

- Job
- *Job* addresses the problem of human suffering. Job, a righteous man, faces immense suffering and questions God's justice. The book ultimately emphasizes the mystery of suffering and the greatness of God's wisdom.
- Psalms
- A collection of religious songs, prayers, and hymns attributed to various authors, including David. Psalms express a wide range of emotions praise, lament, thanksgiving, and pleas for God's intervention.
- Proverbs
- This book offers wisdom literature, filled with moral sayings, instructions, and teachings primarily attributed to Solomon. It focuses on the importance of wisdom, knowledge, and reverence for God.
- Ecclesiastes
- *Ecclesiastes* reflects on the meaning of life, human pursuits, and the ultimate futility of material wealth and earthly achievements. The book emphasizes vanity and the need for a relationship with God.
- Song of Solomon
- A poetic dialogue that celebrates love and romantic relationships. It is often interpreted as a metaphor for God's love for His people.
- Isaiah
- *Isaiah* contains prophecies about judgment and restoration, detailing the fate of Israel and the nations, the coming of a Messiah, and God's future kingdom of peace.
- Jeremiah
- The prophet Jeremiah speaks of the impending judgment

on Judah, the destruction of Jerusalem, and the promise of a new covenant. His messages are both warnings and promises of hope.

- Lamentations
- *Lamentations* is a poetic reflection on the destruction of Jerusalem, lamenting the suffering of the people and the city, but also expressing hope for restoration.
- Ezekiel
- *Ezekiel* contains visions of divine judgment and restoration. It speaks of the destruction of Israel's enemies and the eventual return of the exiles and the rebuilding of the Temple.
- Daniel
- The book contains visions of future kingdoms and apocalyptic themes, including the famous story of Daniel in the lion's den and the interpretation of King Nebuchadnezzar's dream.
- Hosea
- *Hosea* uses the prophet's troubled marriage to an unfaithful wife as a metaphor for God's relationship with Israel, focusing on themes of love, repentance, and restoration.
- Joel
- *Joel* speaks of divine judgment on Israel and the nations and prophesies the coming of the Spirit of God upon all people.
- Amos
- Amos is a prophetic book that emphasizes social justice, God's judgment on Israel, and the need for the nation to repent. Amos condemns the wealthy and corrupt leaders of Israel for their exploitation of the poor and oppressed, calling for true righteousness and justice.
- Obadiah

- Obadiah is the shortest book in the Old Testament and focuses on the destruction of Edom. The prophet declares that God will bring judgment upon Edom for its arrogance and betrayal of Israel, and the book ends with a vision of Israel's ultimate restoration.
- Jonah
- The book of Jonah tells the story of the prophet Jonah, who is sent by God to the city of Nineveh to call its people to repentance. Jonah's reluctance to follow God's command and his eventual mission to Nineveh highlights God's mercy and compassion for all nations, not just Israel.
- Micah
- Micah is a prophetic book that warns of judgment against Israel and Judah for their sins, particularly their corruption and exploitation of the poor. The book also contains messages of hope, promising that a future ruler, a descendant of David, will bring peace and restoration to the people.
- Nahum
- Nahum focuses on the fall of Nineveh, the capital of the Assyrian Empire. The book describes the city's impending destruction and God's justice for its violence and idolatry. It serves as a reminder of God's sovereignty over the nations.
- Habakkuk
- Habakkuk addresses the prophet's questions about the problem of evil and suffering, as he struggles to understand why God allows wickedness to flourish. The book ends with a declaration of faith, emphasizing that the righteous shall live by faith.
- Zephaniah
- Zephaniah prophesies the coming day of the Lord, a time when God will bring judgment upon Judah and the nations

for their idolatry and sin. However, the book also holds out hope for a remnant of people who will seek God in humility and be restored.

- Haggai
- Haggai is a post-exilic book that encourages the Israelites to rebuild the Temple in Jerusalem after their return from Babylonian exile. The book highlights the importance of obedience to God's commands and the restoration of worship.
- Zechariah
- Zechariah contains a series of visions and prophecies concerning the rebuilding of Jerusalem and the coming of a future Messianic kingdom. The book's visions include symbolic representations of the Messiah, the rebuilding of the Temple, and the ultimate victory of God over evil.
- Malachi
- The final book of the Old Testament, Malachi, addresses the spiritual and moral decline of Israel after the exile. The book contains prophecies of the coming of Elijah and the Messiah, urging the people to return to faithfulness and righteousness.

## The Apocryphal Books

- 1 Esdras
- This book is an expanded version of the Book of Ezra, telling the story of the return from Babylonian exile and the rebuilding of the Temple in Jerusalem. It offers additional historical details and emphasizes the importance of God's covenant.
- Tobit

- Tobit tells the story of Tobit, a righteous man who faces adversity, and his son Tobias, who embarks on a journey to recover a debt. The book emphasizes God's providence, faith, and divine intervention.
- Judith
- Judith is the story of a widow who saves Israel from an enemy invasion through her courage and faith in God. Her actions exemplify divine deliverance and the power of faithful women in the Bible.
- The Wisdom of Sirach (Ecclesiasticus)
- This book is a collection of wise sayings and ethical teachings that reflect on the importance of wisdom, morality, and devotion to God. It highlights the relationship between wisdom and righteous living, and its message echoes themes from Proverbs.
- Baruch
- Baruch, attributed to the scribe of Jeremiah, is a book of prayers and confessions. It calls on the Israelites to return to God and offers hope for restoration following their exile.
- The Letter of Jeremiah
- This brief letter was written to the exiled Israelites in Babylon, urging them to avoid the idolatry of the Babylonians and remain faithful to God. It emphasizes the futility of idols and the greatness of the one true God.
- The Prayer of Azariah and the Song of the Three Youths
- This addition to the Book of Daniel tells the story of the three youths Shadrach, Meshach, and Abednego who refuse to worship the golden idol and are thrown into the fiery furnace. The prayer and song they recite emphasize their faithfulness to God.
- Susanna

- The story of Susanna, falsely accused of adultery, showcases the power of divine justice and the importance of innocence and truth. It highlights the theme of God's protection and vindication of the righteous.
- Bel and the Dragon
- This addition to Daniel highlights Daniel's triumph over the false idols and deceptive practices of the Babylonian king, demonstrating God's power over all forms of idolatry.
- 1 Maccabees
- 1 Maccabees narrates the story of the Maccabean revolt, where the Jewish people fought to reclaim their religious freedom and restore the Temple in Jerusalem. It focuses on the importance of faithful resistance to oppression and the restoration of true worship.
- 2 Maccabees
- 2 Maccabees complements the story in 1 Maccabees, emphasizing the spiritual lessons of the Maccabean revolt. It highlights the importance of prayer and dedication to God in the face of suffering and adversity.
- The Book of Enoch
- The Book of Enoch is one of the most significant and influential texts in the Ethiopian canon. It focuses on the watchers, fallen angels who descend to earth and corrupt humanity, leading to divine judgment. It offers an apocalyptic vision and themes of justice, redemption, and cosmic struggle.
- Jubilees
- Often called the "Little Genesis," Jubilees offers a retelling of the Book of Genesis and Exodus, emphasizing the importance of divine law and obedience to God. It presents the history of the world in jubilee cycles, focusing on the covenant between God and His people.

· The Ascension of Isaiah
· The Ascension of Isaiah describes the prophet Isaiah's vision
  of heaven and the events leading to his death. The text
  blends prophecy, apocalyptic visions, and early Christian
  Christology, emphasizing the coming of the Messiah and
  His heavenly glory.

**The New Testament**

· The Gospel of Matthew
· Summary: Matthew's Gospel presents Jesus as the Messiah
  who fulfills the prophecies of the Old Testament. The book
  focuses on Jesus' teachings, particularly the Sermon on the
  Mount, and His role as the King of the Jews.
· Key Characters & Stories: Jesus Christ, the Apostles, the Sermon on the Mount, The Birth of Jesus, and The Crucifixion
  and Resurrection.
· Theological Implications: Matthew's Gospel emphasizes
  the fulfillment of the Law and prophecy in Jesus, highlighting themes of obedience to God's commandments and the
  coming of God's kingdom.
· The Gospel of Mark
· Summary: The shortest of the four Gospels, Mark's account
  focuses on the action and miracles of Jesus. It presents Jesus
  as a suffering servant, emphasizing His sacrifice and the
  cost of discipleship.
· Key Characters & Stories: Jesus Christ, Peter, the Twelve
  Apostles, miracles, parables, and the Passion of Christ.
· Theological Implications: Mark's Gospel highlights Jesus'
  authority over sin, sickness, and death, and presents the
  suffering Messiah as central to Christian faith and salvation.

- The Gospel of Luke
- Summary: Luke's Gospel provides a detailed account of Jesus' life, focusing on His compassion for the marginalized, such as the poor, women, and sinners. Luke emphasizes the universal nature of the gospel and the importance of love and forgiveness.
- Key Characters & Stories: Jesus Christ, Mary, the Good Samaritan parable, the Prodigal Son, Zacchaeus, and the Resurrection.
- Theological Implications: Luke's Gospel highlights divine compassion and the salvation of all peoples, emphasizing social justice, repentance, and God's mercy.
- The Gospel of John
- Summary: John's Gospel presents a deeply theological view of Jesus, focusing on His divine nature as the Son of God. The book contains profound discourses about Jesus as the Word (Logos) made flesh and the source of eternal life.
- Key Characters & Stories: Jesus Christ, Nicodemus, The Woman at the Well, The Raising of Lazarus, The Last Supper, and Jesus' Passion.
- Theological Implications: John's Gospel emphasizes the divinity of Christ, the eternal life He offers, and the necessity of believing in Him to receive salvation. It highlights Christ as the Light of the World and the path to reconciliation with God.
- Acts of the Apostles (Book 58)
- Acts of the Apostles
- Summary: Written by Luke, Acts tells the story of the early Church after Jesus' ascension. It covers the spread of Christianity through the missions of Peter and Paul, the coming of the Holy Spirit, and the struggles of the early

Christian community.

- Key Characters & Stories: Peter, Paul, the Apostles, Pentecost, the conversion of Saul (Paul), missionary journeys, and persecutions.
- Theological Implications: Acts emphasizes the work of the Holy Spirit in empowering the apostles, the church's mission to spread the gospel to the Gentiles, and the unity of the Church across cultural and ethnic lines.
- Pauline Epistles (Books 59-78)
- Romans
- Summary: In this foundational epistle, Paul explains the doctrine of justification by faith and the role of grace in salvation. He addresses the relationship between Jews and Gentiles and teaches about living in the Spirit.
- Key Characters & Stories: Paul, the Roman Christians, Abraham, and the Holy Spirit.
- Theological Implications: Romans introduces the concept of justification by faith and explores the depth of God's grace, salvation, and the life in Christ.
- 1 Corinthians
- Summary: Paul addresses division in the Church at Corinth, emphasizing unity in Christ. He speaks about spiritual gifts, love, and resurrection.
- Key Characters & Stories: Paul, the Corinthian Church, spiritual gifts, the Lord's Supper, and resurrection.
- Theological Implications: This letter focuses on the importance of unity in the body of Christ, spiritual maturity, and the centrality of love in Christian life.
- 2 Corinthians
- Summary: Paul defends his apostolic authority and emphasizes the comfort Christians find in Christ. He also speaks

about the ministry of reconciliation and the treasure in jars of clay.

- Key Characters & Stories: Paul, the Corinthian Church, comfort in affliction, and the ministry of reconciliation.
- Theological Implications: 2 Corinthians speaks to the comfort Christians find in suffering, the power of God working through human weakness, and the role of the Church in reconciling the world to God.
- Galatians
- Summary: Paul addresses the issue of circumcision and the law, asserting that salvation comes by faith, not works of the law. He emphasizes the freedom in Christ and the role of the Holy Spirit.
- Key Characters & Stories: Paul, the Galatians, and the Judaizers.
- Theological Implications: Galatians emphasizes freedom in Christ, the outworking of the Spirit, and justification by faith alone.
- Ephesians
- Summary: Paul speaks about the unity of the Church in Christ and the spiritual blessings that believers have. He discusses Christian living and the importance of armor of God in spiritual warfare.
- Key Characters & Stories: Paul, the Ephesians, and the Church's unity in Christ.
- Theological Implications: Ephesians highlights the universal Church, spiritual growth, and spiritual warfare.
- Philippians
- Summary: Paul writes with joy and thanksgiving to the Philippians, encouraging them to rejoice in the Lord and live with humility, following Christ's example.

- Key Characters & Stories: Paul, the Philippians, and Christ's humility.
- Theological Implications: Philippians focuses on joy in Christ, humility, and contentment in all circumstances.
- Colossians
- Summary: Paul emphasizes the supremacy of Christ and urges the Colossians to live in a manner worthy of their calling. He also deals with false teachings and encourages Christian virtues.
- Key Characters & Stories: Paul, the Colossians, and the supremacy of Christ.
- Theological Implications: Colossians speaks about the cosmic authority of Christ and the new life that Christians have in Him.
- 1 Thessalonians
- Summary: Paul encourages the Thessalonian Church to continue in faith and holiness, while addressing concerns about the return of Christ and the resurrection.
- Key Characters & Stories: Paul, the Thessalonians, and the second coming of Christ.
- Theological Implications: 1 Thessalonians emphasizes hope in the return of Christ and living faithfully until He comes.
- 2 Thessalonians
- Summary: Paul encourages the Thessalonians to stand firm in their faith, even in the face of persecution. He provides clarity on the second coming of Christ and end times events.
- Key Characters & Stories: Paul, the Thessalonians, and the second coming of Christ.
- Theological Implications: This letter focuses on end times theology, faith under persecution, and the certainty of Christ's return.

- 1 Timothy
- Summary: Paul writes to Timothy, giving guidance on church leadership, the role of elders and deacons, and the importance of sound doctrine.
- Key Characters & Stories: Paul, Timothy, and the qualifications for leaders.
- Theological Implications: 1 Timothy emphasizes the importance of leadership, sound doctrine, and godly conduct in the Church.
- 2 Timothy
- Summary: Paul writes his final letter to Timothy, urging him to persevere in the faith, despite trials and persecution. Paul speaks of the importance of Scripture and the role of preaching.
- Key Characters & Stories: Paul, Timothy, and the call to endure.
- Theological Implications: 2 Timothy speaks to the endurance required for faithful ministry and the vital role of the Scriptures in sustaining the Church.
- Titus
- Summary: Paul writes to Titus, instructing him on the role of church leaders, sound doctrine, and the importance of good works as an expression of faith.
- Key Characters & Stories: Paul, Titus, and the qualifications for church leadership.
- Theological Implications: Titus focuses on church leadership and the need for good works in the Christian community.
- Philemon
- Summary: Paul writes to Philemon, urging him to forgive his runaway slave, Onesimus, who has become a Christian.

This letter highlights the themes of forgiveness and reconciliation.

- Key Characters & Stories: Paul, Philemon, Onesimus, and forgiveness.
- Theological Implications: Philemon emphasizes Christian reconciliation and forgiving others in the family of faith.
- Hebrews
- Summary: The Book of Hebrews presents Christ as the ultimate high priest, emphasizing His superiority over the Levitical priesthood. The book explains that Jesus is the fulfillment of the Old Testament sacrificial system and that His sacrifice offers eternal salvation for humanity.
- Key Characters & Stories: Jesus Christ, the high priest, Melchizedek, and the Old Testament heroes of faith.
- Theological Implications: Hebrews explores the new covenant established by Christ, highlighting Christ's priestly role and the eternal nature of His sacrifice. It emphasizes the superiority of Christ over the angels, Moses, and the Old Testament priesthood.
- James
- Summary: James, the brother of Jesus, writes to encourage Christians to live out their faith through good works. The book emphasizes practical Christian living, focusing on issues such as faith and works, wisdom, and patience in suffering.
- *Key Characters & Stories*: James, the Christian community, and the wisdom from above.
- *Theological Implications*: James stresses the importance of living faith faith that is active and demonstrated through righteous deeds. It highlights the relationship between faith and works and calls Christians to humble submission to

God's will.

- 1 Peter
- *Summary*: Written by Peter, this epistle encourages Christians to persevere in their faith and hope despite suffering and persecution. It offers exhortations to holy living and calls the faithful to follow the example of Christ in enduring suffering for the sake of righteousness.
- *Key Characters & Stories*: Peter, the suffering Christians, and Christ as the model of suffering. *Theological Implications*: 1 Peter emphasizes Christian endurance in the face of trials and calls believers to be holy and set apart. It highlights Christ's redemptive suffering and the idea that suffering for Christ leads to spiritual transformation and future glory.
- 2 Peter
- *Summary*: 2 Peter addresses false teachers who have infiltrated the Christian community, encouraging believers to remain steadfast in the true knowledge of Christ. The book also focuses on the certainty of Christ's return and the final judgment.
- *Key Characters & Stories*: Peter, false teachers, and the promise of Christ's return.
- *Theological Implications*: 2 Peter warns about the dangers of false teachings, urging believers to grow in their knowledge of Christ and live according to His word.
- 2 John
- *Summary*: 2 John is a brief letter that warns against deceptive teachers and encourages the Christian community to walk in truth and love.
- *Key Characters & Stories*: John, the chosen lady, and false teachers.
- *Theological Implications*: 2 John reinforces the importance of

truth in the Christian walk and the need for doctrinal purity. It calls Christians to love one another while rejecting false teachings that distort the gospel.

- 3 John
- *Summary*: 3 John is a personal letter to a believer named Gaius, commending him for his hospitality to Christian travelers and warning him about Diotrephes, a church leader who refused to welcome John's emissaries.
- *Key Characters & Stories*: John, Gaius, and Diotrephes.
- *Theological Implications*: 3 John highlights the importance of hospitality, faithful leadership, and walking in truth. It also addresses the issue of church discipline and the need for spiritual unity.
- Jude
- *Summary*: Jude, the brother of Jesus, writes to warn Christians about false teachers who are distorting the faith. He calls on believers to contend for the faith and remain faithful to God's truth.
- *Key Characters & Stories*: Jude, false teachers, and the faithful believers.
- *Theological Implications*: Jude stresses the need for vigilance against false teachings and the importance of remaining firm in the true gospel. He also speaks about God's judgment on the wicked and encourages believers to keep themselves in God's love.
- Revelation (The Apocalypse of John)
- *Summary*: The final book of the Bible, *Revelation*, is a prophetic vision given to John that describes the ultimate victory of Christ over evil, the coming of God's kingdom, and the final judgment of the world.
- *Key Characters & Stories*: Jesus Christ, the angels, the Beast,

the Antichrist, and the New Jerusalem.

- *Theological Implications*: *Revelation* emphasizes God's sovereignty, the coming of Christ's kingdom, and the hope of eternal life. It challenges believers to remain faithful in the face of persecution and assures them that Christ's victory over evil is certain.
- The Shepherd of Hermas
- *Summary*: A Christian writing that addresses themes of repentance, holiness, and Christian conduct. The book uses allegory and visions to convey its messages about spiritual renewal and the importance of obedience to God's will.
- *Key Characters & Stories*: Hermas, the shepherd, and his visions of repentance.
- *Theological Implications*: The Shepherd of Hermas stresses spiritual renewal through repentance and calls Christians to lead lives of purity and holiness while waiting for the second coming of Christ.
- The Epistle of Barnabas
- *Summary*: The Epistle of Barnabas is an early Christian work that provides a Christian interpretation of the Old Testament and stresses the new covenant in Christ. It critiques Jewish customs and promotes Christian liberty.
- *Key Characters & Stories*: Barnabas, the Church, and the new covenant.
- *Theological Implications*: This epistle emphasizes the spiritual nature of the law and argues that Christians should live by faith rather than adhere to the Old Testament law.

*Key Characters and Stories: Highlights of the Major Figures and Stories That Make the Ethiopian Bible Unique*

While many of the figures in the Ethiopian Bible mirror those in the wider Christian canon, the **extra-biblical books** especially those in the Ethiopian canon highlight several key figures and narratives that are unique to Ethiopian Christianity. For instance, **Enoch** and the **Queen of Sheba** are central figures not only in Ethiopia's religious history but also in its identity as a nation chosen by God. The **Queen of Sheba's** visit to King Solomon is considered one of the most significant events in Ethiopia's biblical legacy, further legitimizing Ethiopia's **royal line** as a divinely appointed one.

Additionally, **St. Tekle Haymanot**, **St. Yared**, and **St. Abbo** are vital figures in Ethiopian religious history. These saints' stories often intertwine with **biblical narratives**, showing their miraculous deeds and their deep spiritual connection to God.

*Theological Implications: Analysis of Key Theological Points from Each Book*

The Ethiopian Bible's unique selection of books offers significant theological insights. **The Book of Enoch**, for example, introduces a **cosmic view** of sin, judgment, and the divine order that emphasizes the role of angels and the heavenly realms in the divine plan. **Jubilees** stresses the importance of **divine law** and obedience, revealing God's desire for His people to walk in faithfulness to His commandments. These works, while apocryphal, provide a **theological depth** that shapes the Ethiopian Church's understanding of holiness, righteousness, and salvation.

Each book in the Ethiopian Bible contributes to a larger, **theologically rich narrative** about humanity's relationship with God, the role of divine law, and the ultimate restoration of creation. It is through these additional books, alongside the well-known canonical texts, that the Ethiopian Bible offers **a fuller vision of salvation** one that includes both divine judgment and a promise of redemption for all people.

# Chapter 9

## The Ethiopian Bible in Contemporary Christianity

G lobal Impact: *How the Ethiopian Bible is Influencing Modern Christian Thought, Especially in the Context of African Christianity*

The Ethiopian Bible plays a significant role in the development of modern Christian thought, especially within the context of African Christianity. For centuries, Ethiopia has been a spiritual beacon of Christianity, with the Ethiopian Orthodox Church preserving its unique canon of 88 books and rich theological traditions. In recent years, the global interest in the Ethiopian Bible has deepened, particularly as African Christianity seeks to reclaim its spiritual identity and rediscover its ancient roots.

The Ethiopian Bible's inclusion of apocryphal books such as The Book of Enoch, Jubilees, and 1 Maccabees offers a broader theological framework that contrasts with the more streamlined canons of Protestant and Catholic traditions. These additional texts allow African Christians to explore the diverse theological perspectives that were present in the early Church, showing that Christianity in Africa was deeply connected to the ancient Christian world long before European colonialism introduced Western theological concepts.

One major area where the Ethiopian Bible is influencing African Christianity is in its focus on community-oriented worship and holistic spirituality. African Christians often have a strong sense of communal identity, and the Ethiopian Bible's emphasis on the spiritual well-being of the community, rather than just the individual, resonates deeply with these values. The rituals, prayers, and liturgies surrounding the Ethiopian Bible encourage a sense of collective faith and participation in the divine life, which aligns with the African worldview that emphasizes family, tradition, and the community's role in the faith journey.

Moreover, the Ethiopian Bible's focus on justice, divine mercy, and salvation has provided a theological platform for addressing modern social issues such as poverty, inequality, and political unrest. Ethiopian Christianity's social gospel speaks to the moral responsibility of Christians to not only focus on personal salvation but also to engage in the transformation of society. In this context, the Ethiopian Bible serves as a guiding light for African Christians who are seeking to confront the complex challenges faced by their communities in the modern world.

*Revival of Interest: The Growing Interest in the Ethiopian Bible Among Scholars and Laypeople*

In recent decades, there has been a revival of interest in the Ethiopian Bible, with both scholars and laypeople increasingly turning to this ancient text as a valuable resource for understanding early Christian history and theology. This growing interest reflects a broader desire to reconnect with the roots of Christianity and reclaim lost traditions that are often overshadowed by more dominant Christian narratives from the West.

Scholars of biblical studies, theology, and church history have increasingly focused on the Ethiopian Bible's canon, recognizing its importance in the development of Christian doctrine and theological diversity. Many scholars are now exploring the historical context in which these additional books were written and examining how they contribute to biblical theology. The Book of Enoch, for example, has sparked renewed interest in apocalyptic literature and angelology, offering fresh perspectives on heavenly realms, divine judgment, and the role of angels in Christian thought.

For laypeople, the Ethiopian Bible has become a gateway to a deeper understanding of their own Christian heritage. Ethiopian Christians, in particular, are rediscovering the richness of their faith as preserved in these ancient texts. The Ethiopian Orthodox Church, with its centuries-old tradition of preserving these sacred writings, continues to inspire Ethiopian Christians and African Christians more broadly to delve deeper into their biblical heritage.

The translation of the Ethiopian Bible into modern languages, such as English, French, and Arabic, has also played a crucial role in making the text accessible to a wider audience. Online platforms, digital archives, and academic publications are making these texts more available for global study, allowing people around the world to engage with the spiritual teachings and theological insights contained in the Ethiopian Bible.

*Ethiopian Bible and Interfaith Dialogue: How the Ethiopian Bible is Contributing to Dialogue Between Different Christian Denomina-*

*tions and Religions*

The Ethiopian Bible's unique status as a preserver of early Christian traditions has made it an important tool in interfaith dialogue, not only between different Christian denominations but also between Christianity and other religions. Its rich theological heritage, inclusion of apocryphal books, and its unique spiritual practices offer insights into the diverse ways Christianity has been understood and practiced throughout history.

In inter-denominational dialogue, the Ethiopian Bible has become a point of interest, especially as scholars from various Christian traditions (Catholic, Protestant, Orthodox) seek to understand the wider biblical landscape. The inclusion of books such as The Book of Enoch, Jubilees, and 1 Maccabees invites dialogue about the early formation of the Christian canon and how it relates to Jewish traditions. This has led to more inclusive conversations about the development of biblical doctrine, sacred texts, and the role of tradition in shaping Christian beliefs.

The theological richness of the Ethiopian Bible also makes it an excellent resource for Christian-Muslim dialogue. Both religions share a common interest in the Old Testament and the prophetic traditions, and the Ethiopian Bible's inclusion of certain apocryphal texts that overlap with Islamic traditions (such as the Book of Enoch and the story of the Queen of Sheba) provides a fertile ground for conversation and mutual understanding. For instance, the Queen of Sheba's visit to Solomon, an important story in the Ethiopian Bible, is also referenced in Islamic tradition, where the Queen is considered a figure of wisdom and faith.

The Ethiopian Bible's emphasis on divine justice, mercy, and the universal nature of God's love is an important theological bridge between Christianity and other world religions. Its inclusion of teachings that align with the ethical principles found in both Judaism and Islam—such as the importance of social justice, holiness, and ethical living—makes it a valuable tool for interfaith understanding. The concept of the Kingdom of God as presented in the Ethiopian Bible also resonates with the eschatological views in Judaism and Islam, opening the door for deeper dialogue on the end times and divine salvation.

Furthermore, the Ethiopian Bible's emphasis on intercession by saints and the role of angels invites dialogue within Christianity itself, especially concerning differences in doctrines of salvation, saintly intercession, and the role of the Virgin Mary in the Christian tradition. The Ethiopian Orthodox Church places a significant emphasis on the intercession of saints and the veneration of Mary, which contrasts with the Protestant emphasis on sola scriptura (scripture alone) and Christ as the sole mediator.

Through its unique theological perspective and its deep connection to early Christian history, the Ethiopian Bible has the potential to bridge gaps between different Christian denominations and foster greater mutual understanding between Christianity and other world religions.

# Chapter 10

Practical Applications and Lessons from the Ethiopian Bible

*Living the Teachings: Practical Advice Based on the Ethiopian Bible's Teachings for Modern Believers*

The Ethiopian Bible is not just a historical text or theological guide; it is a **living document** that continues to offer **practical wisdom** and **guidance** for modern believers. Its teachings, drawn from both the **Old Testament** and the **apocryphal books**, provide timeless lessons on how to live a righteous life, navigate trials, and maintain a relationship with God.

- **Faithfulness to God's Word**
- One of the central themes throughout the Ethiopian Bible is the importance of **obedience** and **faithfulness** to God's commandments. In the **Old Testament**, the Israelites are consistently reminded of the covenant God made with them. The teachings of the **prophets** emphasize the need for repentance, prayer, and **faithfulness** to God's laws,

which can be directly applied to believers today. Just as the **Israelites** were instructed to love God with all their heart, soul, and mind, modern Christians are called to make God the center of their lives. This foundational message teaches believers the importance of **staying committed** to God even in the face of challenges and distractions.

· **Holiness in Daily Life**
· The **wisdom literature** in the Ethiopian Bible, such as the **Book of Proverbs** and **Sirach**, provides guidance on living with **integrity**, **honesty**, and **humility**. These books emphasize that **wisdom** is not merely intellectual knowledge but a moral compass that directs how one interacts with others, how one treats the poor, and how one maintains justice. Modern believers can take these teachings and apply them by striving for **holiness** in their personal lives, relationships, work, and communities. **Integrity**, **purity**, and **humility** are timeless virtues that contribute to a strong, ethical foundation for any believer.

· **Social Justice and Compassion**
· The Ethiopian Bible offers **practical advice** on caring for the **marginalized**, **poor**, and **oppressed**. Books like **Isaiah**, **Jeremiah**, and the **Book of Enoch** address the importance of **social justice** and condemning the exploitation of the vulnerable. The **New Testament**, especially in the **Gospels** and **Acts**, emphasizes the call to love one's neighbor and to show compassion to the **suffering**. This message calls modern believers to engage in **acts of mercy**, **serve others**, and work towards creating just and compassionate societies. The Ethiopian Bible's emphasis on **mercy** and **justice** encourages believers to advocate for **fair treatment** of all people, especially those who are marginalized or oppressed.

*Meditation and Prayer: Using the Ethiopian Bible for Daily
Devotion, Prayer, and Spiritual Growth*

The Ethiopian Bible is a powerful tool for **daily devotion** and
**spiritual growth**. With its **rich spiritual heritage** and **depth of
wisdom**, the Ethiopian Bible provides abundant material for
**meditation**, **prayer**, and **reflection**. Its unique combination
of **biblical teachings**, **poetic prayers**, and **prophetic visions**
allows believers to immerse themselves in spiritual practices
that **strengthen their faith** and **deepen their connection to God**.

- **Daily Meditation on Scripture**
- The Ethiopian Bible offers a wealth of **scriptural passages**
  that can be used for **meditation**. Whether reading from the
  **Psalms**, which express every range of human emotion from
  praise to lament, or from the **wisdom books** like **Proverbs**
  and **Sirach**, believers can reflect on God's word and find
  practical guidance for their day-to-day lives. **Scripture
  memorization** is encouraged, especially in the Ethiopian
  Orthodox tradition, as it allows believers to keep God's
  word close to their hearts. Passages such as the **Lord's
  Prayer** or the **Beatitudes** provide powerful reminders of
  God's **kingdom values**, while the **apocryphal books**, like
  **The Wisdom of Sirach**, offer wisdom on living virtuously
  and justly.
- **Prayer and Worship**
- Prayer is central to the Ethiopian Christian life, and the
  Ethiopian Bible provides ample material for **devotional
  prayer**. The Psalms, with their poetic beauty, serve as a great
  model for **praise**, **adoration**, and **confession**. The **prayers
  of the saints**, such as the prayers of **Daniel**, **Esther**, and

**Manasseh**, offer examples of how to approach God in times of **suffering** or **repentance**. **Jesus' own prayers**, as recorded in the Gospels, also offer a model of **humility, submission to God's will**, and **dependence on God**. Ethiopian Christians often engage in regular **liturgical prayer** and **chanting**, emphasizing the importance of communal prayer for both personal and collective growth.

· **Spiritual Fasting and Disciplines**
· Fasting is another key practice in the Ethiopian Orthodox Church, which uses both **the Old Testament** and **New Testament** teachings to support the **spiritual discipline** of fasting. The **fasting seasons**, such as **Lent**, help believers prepare spiritually and emotionally for the **celebration of Easter**. In the Ethiopian Bible, the **prophets** and **Jesus** Himself call for times of **fasting, prayer**, and **repentance** to draw closer to God. Fasting is seen as a way to **discipline the body** and focus more intently on **spiritual growth**, providing clarity, humility, and a greater dependence on God.

*A Call for Unity and Peace: How the Ethiopian Bible's Messages Can Help Address Contemporary Social Issues*

The Ethiopian Bible is a powerful call for **unity** and **peace**, both within the Church and the wider world. Its message of **social justice**, **mercy**, and **reconciliation** speaks directly to contemporary social issues, encouraging believers to be **peacemakers**, to foster **unity**, and to work toward a world that reflects **God's kingdom** on earth.

· **Building Unity in the Body of Christ**
· One of the main theological themes of the Ethiopian Bible

is **unity in the Church**. Despite the historical divisions in Christian denominations, the Ethiopian Bible calls Christians to find common ground in the **central message of Christ**, which transcends **doctrinal differences**. The **New Testament**, especially in the epistles of **Paul**, calls Christians to **love one another**, **forgive each other**, and **embrace peace**. The Ethiopian Bible's **teachings** on love, **faith**, and **forgiveness** encourage contemporary Christians to **build unity** in their local churches and communities, emphasizing that, despite differences, all believers are united in **Christ**.

· **Addressing Modern Social Injustices**

· The Ethiopian Bible has long been a **spiritual resource** for addressing **social injustices** such as **poverty**, **inequality**, and **oppression**. The Old Testament prophets spoke of **divine justice** and God's concern for the **poor** and **marginalized**. The **Gospels** and **Paul's letters** call for **justice**, **equality**, and **helping the needy**, with specific instructions on how to treat the **oppressed**. In today's world, the Ethiopian Bible serves as a moral compass to **guide Christians** in addressing issues such as **racial inequality**, **economic disparities**, and **violence**. The teachings of the Ethiopian Bible can provide a framework for **Christians to engage in social justice**, acting as **agents of peace** and advocates for those without a voice.

· **Promoting Peace in a Divided World**

· The Ethiopian Bible's focus on **peace** and **reconciliation** is especially relevant in today's divided world. Whether addressing **religious conflict**, **political polarization**, or **ethnic tensions**, the Bible's teachings encourage believers to act as **peacemakers**. The **Sermon on the Mount**, found in the **Gospels**, presents a radical message of **nonviolence** and **forgiveness**, calling Christians to love their enemies and seek peace. The **prophets** in the Ethiopian Bible emphasize **God's desire for peace** among His people and urge Christians to **follow His example** by pursuing peace in their relationships with others. The Ethiopian Bible can serve as a powerful resource for fostering **reconciliation**, urging believers to seek **peace** in their communities and the world.

# Conclusion

## Embracing the Wisdom of the Ethiopian Bible

*The Eternal Relevance of the Ethiopian Bible: A Reflection on the Timeless Nature of the Bible's Teachings*

T he Ethiopian Bible, with its 88 books, presents a vision of Christian faith that is both ancient and ever-relevant. Its teachings transcend time and culture, offering wisdom that speaks to the hearts and minds of believers across generations. From its **prophetic insights** to its **spiritual guidance**, the Ethiopian Bible invites all who read it to reflect on the eternal **truths** of **divine justice**, **mercy**, and **grace**. Whether one is seeking answers to the **questions of life**, or striving to live a life more aligned with **God's will**, the Ethiopian Bible offers a rich **spiritual treasury** that continues to resonate with **modern believers**.

In a world that often feels fractured and uncertain, the Ethiopian Bible's **message of unity**, **peace**, and **faithfulness** is a reminder that God's **word** remains a source of **hope** and **strength** in every season of life. The message of **salvation** through Jesus Christ, which runs through both its **Old Testament** and **New Testament** books, speaks to the universal **human condition**, addressing both personal and communal struggles. The Bible's lessons about **justice**, **forgiveness**, and **spiritual transformation** continue to challenge and inspire those who seek to follow the path of **righteousness** and **peace**.

## The Journey of Discovery: Encouraging Readers to Continue Exploring the Depths of the Ethiopian Bible and Its Spiritual Richness

The Ethiopian Bible is not simply a text to be read once and set aside. It is a **living document**, full of **mystery**, **depth**, and **spiritual insight** that rewards ongoing exploration. Whether you are a **new reader** or someone who has long embraced the teachings of the Ethiopian Church, there is always more to discover. The **apocryphal books**, the **prophetic visions**, and the **wisdom literature** all invite the reader into a **journey of discovery**—a journey that never truly ends but deepens as one matures in their **spiritual walk**.

The more one immerses themselves in these ancient texts, the more one can experience their **transformational power**. The Ethiopian Bible speaks not just to the **intellect**, but to the **heart and spirit**, offering profound insights into the nature of God, humanity, and the **sacred mission** of the Church. **Daily meditation**, **prayer**, and **reflection** on the Ethiopian Bible can illuminate life's **challenges**, offer comfort in times of distress, and inspire one to live out the **divine calling** with integrity and joy.

Encouraging readers to engage continually with the Bible, to ponder its teachings, and to apply its wisdom to **real-life situations**, this journey of discovery will lead to an ever-deepening

**relationship with God**. The Ethiopian Bible's rich **spiritual heritage** provides a pathway to growth—both in knowledge and in **Christlike character**—making it an invaluable tool for all Christians, especially in today's world.

*Call to Action: A Final Message to Readers to Engage More Deeply with the Ethiopian Bible and Its Teachings in Their Own Faith Journey*

As you conclude your exploration of the Ethiopian Bible in this book, consider this not as an end, but a **beginning**. The **wisdom** contained within its pages is not just for academic study or historical reflection, but for **daily living**. I encourage you to **continue your journey** with the Ethiopian Bible, using it as a guide to deepen your relationship with God, enhance your spiritual practices, and live out the teachings of Christ in your community and beyond.

Make **prayer** and **meditation** on the Ethiopian Bible a **daily discipline**, and allow its messages of **faith**, **love**, **forgiveness**, and **justice** to shape the way you engage with the world. Seek out moments of **quiet reflection** on its teachings, and allow these divine words to **transform** how you see God, yourself, and others. Let the lessons of the Ethiopian Bible help you navigate **life's challenges**, encourage you to pursue **holiness**, and inspire you to be a light to those around you.

Ultimately, the Ethiopian Bible is a gift—not just for Ethiopian Christians, but for all Christians who seek a **deeper**, **richer** understanding of God's Word. Its **ancient** yet **timeless** wisdom continues to have a **profound impact** on believers around the world. As you walk this journey of faith, may the Ethiopian Bible guide you, empower you, and lead you closer to the **heart of God**.

# About the Author

**Jordan Elias** is a passionate writer, researcher, and theologian with a deep interest in the history and theology of early Christianity. With years of study in both **biblical scholarship** and **church history**, Jordan has dedicated much of his life to exploring ancient Christian texts and their relevance in modern faith. His works aim to bridge the gap between historical scholarship and practical Christian living, offering readers accessible insights into the rich spiritual traditions of the early Church.

Jordan's academic background in **biblical studies**, **theology**, and **religious history** has led him to a profound understanding of the **Ethiopian Orthodox Church** and its unique contributions to Christianity. He has written extensively on **Christianity's early history**, the **Ethiopian Bible**, and the development of Christian canon and doctrine. Through his research, Jordan seeks to bring to light the **underrated treasures** of the Ethiopian Christian tradition, promoting an understanding of the faith that is rooted in both history and contemporary application.

When not writing or teaching, Jordan is an avid traveler and a passionate advocate for interfaith dialogue, seeking to promote understanding and respect across different Christian denominations and other religious traditions. He currently resides in **[Location]** and continues to work on projects that explore the intersections of **faith, history**, and **spiritual growth**.

www.ingramcontent.com/pod-product-compliance
Lightning Source LLC
Chambersburg PA
CBHW071024060426
42566CB00006B/145